EZRA LADERMAN

PARTITA

Solo Violin

ED-3872

First printing: March 1993

G. SCHIRMER, Inc.

Distributed by

HL Hal Leonard Publishing Corporation

7777 West Bluemound Road P.O. Box 13819 Milwaukee, WI 53213

Partita was premiered on September 26, 1983 by Elmar Oliveira
on CBS Television "Look Up and Live."

Leonidas Kavakos gave the first concert performance
at Alice Tully Hall, New York City, on February 20, 1990.

duration: ca. 28 minutes

PARTITA

Ezra Laderman

I

4

II

Allegro con spirito (♩ = 160)

6

III

8

IV

V

VI

VII

*these trills, marked *accel.* and/or *rit.*, should speed up and/or slow down as indicated.

VIII

IX

16